40 Days of Easter

Rich Stevenson

40 Days of Easter

*Walking with Jesus
from the Resurrection to the Ascension*

Rich Stevenson

altogether LIFE Series – Volume One

1elevenmedia – The Malachi Network

PO Box 368 – Avalon, NJ – 08202

Order additional copies of 40 Days of Easter at:
www.richstevenson.org

ISBN: 1542816688
ISBN-13: 978-1542816687

DEDICATION

This book is dedicated to the 50+ young leaders and their families that make up The Malachi Network (www.malachinetwork.org). These amazing men and women are serving as missionaries and church planters around the globe. They are end-time witnesses of the gospel, committed to prayer and faithful to give themselves to simple communities that do life together.

Tania and I are beyond grateful to be able to love them deeply and serve their Kingdom ministries.

CONTENTS

Prologue

altogether LIFE is a tool to help get people in God's amazing family together. God doesn't intend that any of us make it on our own. Rugged individualism may be American, but it is not Christian. In God's family, we are called to a whole lot of *"one anothers"*: be kind to one another, love one another, honor one another, confess to one another, etc. In God's Family, we make a Declaration of Interdependence!

This is a primer. That means that it is meant to be simple and basic. I am hoping that it will "prime the pump" so creativity and inspiration flow freely as you study with others. There is also a biological definition for primer that I like: *A short sequence of DNA from which DNA replication initiate.* How about that? I believe **altogether LIFE** can provide some spiritual DNA that is highly reproducible through multiplying groups!

The word altogether means *wholly, to a complete degree, to the full extent*. This is exactly the kind of life Jesus has given you. Look at this promise from Jesus: *The thief comes only to steal and kill and destroy; I have come that they may have life, and have it to the full* (John 10:10). These are the ingredients that are necessary for this kind of full life: The Holy Spirit, prayer, the Bible and Christ-like friends. **altogether LIFE** is meant to be a primer for you to access all of these. I am asking the Lord to place this book into the hands of many who will begin this adventure with a few friends, who will in turn gather some friends and lead them on the same adventure. The possibilities are endless, **altogether LIFE** could spread like a holy virus!

This book is designed to be used in a one on one relationship or in a small group. Each person should read a chapter before gathering with a mentor or group. Each chapter will include the following elements:

Bible Story
Bible Study
Vintage Poetry
Creative Space

As author, I attempted to only write what is necessary. I've prayed that my words will simply be a catalyst for you to hear from Jesus. I am trusting that as you read the short chapters and then study God's Word, heaven will be opened and you will encounter the Risen Lord.

The most important thing is for you is to get with at least one other person and believe God together. Jesus said: *The work of God is this: to believe in the one he has sent* (John 6:29). And He said these words not long after He fed about 20,000 people with one little boy's lunch. Explore the blessings and power of Jesus together. Ask yourself each time you gather: *"What are we believing God for today that only He could do?"*

In volume one of **altogether LIFE**, we focus on the theme: **"40 Days of Easter."** We will walk with Jesus during the 40 days between His resurrection and His ascension.

> *"In my former book, Theophilus, I wrote about all that Jesus began to do and to teach until the day he was taken up to heaven, after giving instructions through the Holy Spirit to the apostles he had chosen. After his suffering, he showed himself to these men and gave many convincing proofs that he was alive. He appeared to them over a period of* ***forty days*** *and spoke about the kingdom of God."* Acts 1:1-3

Let's walk with Jesus for these 40 days and watch him encounter people that loved Him. Let's study His message that He gave them. And by the end of our time together, let's believe that we will experience the same power that raised Jesus from the dead. This is LIFE. . .and you can have **altogether LIFE** with the people who gather for this study.

Leaders Guide

So then, just as you received Christ Jesus as Lord,
continue to live in him, rooted and built up in him,
strengthened in the faith as you were taught,
and overflowing with thankfulness.
Colossians 2:6,7

What are the prerequisites that are necessary to lead an individual or a small group in **altogether LIFE?** Great question! Do you need at least 10 years in the faith? Do you need a degree? An ordination certificate? Completion of a 12 week training course? Charisma? A bona fide teaching gift? No, to all of these. Two things are probably necessary, maybe three.

First, you need to care. This seems easy, but it must be more difficult than it looks. You need to care that people know Jesus. You need to care that they move from making a decision for Christ to becoming a disciple of Christ. You need to care that they learn to appropriate the enormous resources that they have in the Bible and through the Holy Spirit. You need to care that they become prepared for the events of the last days.

Second, you need to be able to depend on the person and power of the Holy Spirit. He is the Person that is the most valuable player in this endeavor. He is the guest of honor as you meet. He brings the truth of Jesus, the Father's heart and the creative edge of inspiration. You will need an alertness and sensitivity to His leadership.

The last thing that you will need to lead an **altogether LIFE** gathering is a willingness to ask an individual or a small group of friends to come together. This seems daunting; and the fact is, it is. All of us fear rejection to one degree or another. Both of my sons sold books during the summer door to door. The only way to survive is to embrace that you are going to have 30 doors shut in your face before one opens to even listen to you. I admired their tenacity. Asking people to join you in altogether LIFE isn't as hard as selling books door to door. You've got something even better then study books to offer!

Ask Jesus to give you His compassion. Lean in to the Holy Spirit and let Him direct you to the right people. Ask if they would like to study spiritual truth with you. Don't stand too close to the door. And if it gets shut, go to the next one.

When you come together, get to know one another naturally. The best ministry always happens in the context of deep relationships. Ask Jesus to help you become the best listener. This is such a gift to people. Train yourself to pay attention to what is being said without trying to focus on how you are going to respond. Keep your time together light and fun. Eat together if possible. Most spiritual time is spent being way too intense. Believe that the Lord will give you things to bring to your people. And believe that those who gather with you will be blessed with gifts to bring. Even if this is against your nature, go for the arts together. Believe for songs, poems, pictures, etc. Tap into the creative nature of God together. Unleash your imagination and let it connect with the dreams of God. Can you imagine what is possible? What fun!

The text in each chapter is usually only a handful of pages. Try to have your friend or your group read it before you meet. But if that doesn't happen, take some time in the beginning to read it, even out loud together. The text is full of scripture and there are passages to focus on. Make sure you dive into the Bible. It has the words that bring life and it comes with the promise that it won't return void. There are some words to a classic hymn (vintage poetry) in each chapter written by someone who experienced God. Let these powerful and poetic words influence your prayers. As you read, study the Bible and pray, keep a pen handy. There is space at the end of each chapter for you to write things that the Lord brings to your mind. Even if it seems like a rabbit trail, write it down. It may make sense in an hour, a day or a week.

There is a non-negotiable in order to be an authentic **altogether LIFE** gathering. You must hold each other accountable to the following values:

Deep	**L**ove
Corporate	**I**ntercession
Biblical	**F**aith
Routine	**E**vangelism

Deep Love—I Peter 4:8— *"Above all, love each other deeply, because love covers over a   multitude of sins."*
Corporate Intercession—Matthew 18:19,20—
"Again, I tell you that if two of you agree about   anything you

ask for, it will be done for you by my Father in heaven. For where two or three   come together in my name, there am I with them."

Biblical Faith—Colossians 2:6,7— *"So then, just as you received Christ Jesus as Lord, continue to   live in Him, rooted and built up in Him, strengthened in the faith as you were taught, and   overflowing with thankfulness."*

Routine Evangelism—Philemon 6— *"I pray that you may be active in sharing your faith, so that   you will have a full understanding of every good thing we have in Christ."*

When you pray together, it's OK to focus on the things that you need. But try to spend an equal amount of time thinking and praying about what God wants in your lives, in your family, your neighborhood, your workplace, your church and your city.

And finally, don't let **altogether LIFE** end. Let it spread virally. Work into your last several meetings the plan to multiply. Begin praying for new friends that each of you can gather and help grow into disciples of Jesus.

Altogether LIFE. . . This is what Jesus came for!

Chapter One: Reality of the Resurrection

Do you know what the top two holidays are in America? If the money that we spend is an indicator of the level at which we celebrate, our top two holidays are Christmas and *Halloween*! Something is not right about that.

I'm convinced that Easter doesn't get the emphasis that it deserves. Christmas gets the 4 weeks of Advent leading up to it, and then 12 days with "golden rings" and "Lords a leapin." Lent gets 40 days for self-denial. Even Memorial Day and Labor Day get a long weekend! Yet we just take one Sunday to celebrate the power of a man who conquered death for all who will believe in Him?

> *"Easter is about the wild delight of God's creative power. . . at least we ought to shout Alleluias instead of murmuring them; we should light every candle in the building instead of only some; we should give every man, woman, child, cat and mouse in the place a candle to hold; we should have a real bonfire; and we should splash water about as we renew our baptism vows. It's*

*about the real Jesus coming out of the real tomb
and getting God's real new creation under way.*

*. . .Easter week itself ought not to be the time
when all the clergy sigh with relief and go on
holiday. It ought to be an eight day festival, with
lots of alleluias and extra hymns and spectacular
anthems. Is it any wonder people find it hard to
believe in the resurrection of Jesus if we don't
throw our hats in the air? Is it any wonder we
find it hard to live the resurrection if we don't do
it exuberantly in our liturgies? Is it any wonder
the world doesn't take much notice if Easter is
celebrated as simply the one-day happy ending
tacked on to forty days of fasting and gloom? It's
long overdue that we took a hard look at how we
keep Easter in Church, at home, in our personal
lives, right through the system.*

*. . .This is our greatest day. We should put the
flags out."*

N. T. Wright: Surprised By Hope

Instead of *emphasis*, Easter has gotten a whole lot of *explanation*. It seems that from the first century to the present man has been doing intellectual cartwheels to explain (or explain away) Christ's resurrection. What we can't explain, we can't contain. And therefore we are not in control. Here are some of the *best* human explanations of the resurrection of Jesus Christ.

#1 Jesus didn't die. He was drugged so that it just looked like He died. When His body was placed in the cool tomb, He came out of His stupor and appeared to have been raised.

Really? (As you read that word, say it to yourself with an incredulous draw.)

Rome was really good at killing people. They were the experts. And do you really believe that the disciples could be fooled by a beaten up, drugged up Messiah? And what about the sealed stone and Roman guards?

#2 Christ's followers encountered someone else that looked like Jesus; maybe His half-brother James.

Really? (A little bit of a sarcastic tone works well too.)

Christ's followers remained convinced that this imposter was Jesus for the whole 40 days? Nada.

#3 Christ only appeared to people that really loved Him. They just *wanted* Him to be alive. It was wishful thinking.

Really? (To really sound incredulous, it helps if you press your lips together, lower your eyebrows and squint your eyes.)

What about Thomas? And then later, what about Saul who would become Paul? We all know about Thomas' doubt and Saul was focused on killing Christians! Wishful thinking? Give me a break!

#4 What Christ's followers saw was a vision of a past loved one. Many people see ghosts or spirits of people that they loved.

Really? (You are really getting the hang of this!)

The early followers of Jesus had language for seeing a ghost. Remember what they said when Jesus walked out to them on the water? Their response to seeing Jesus was not *"We have seen a ghost."* It was *"We have seen Jesus and He is risen from the dead!"* That's pretty clear.

#5 The disciples stole Jesus body and made the whole resurrection thing up.

Really? (This time add a great big "O come on!")

First of all, how do you explain that the linen His body was wrapped in was still in the tomb? Did one of the disciples offer this idea before they took Him: *"Hey, we should carry Him naked."* That's not going to happen. And secondly, do you really believe that those eleven men could keep their story together for the rest of their lives?

If Jesus isn't alive, how do you explain that there is no celebrated tomb?

If Jesus isn't alive, how do you explain the sudden willingness to worship on the first day of the week? That was a work day for them. They got together to worship on Sunday before work in the 1st century!

If Jesus isn't alive, how do you explain that his followers were willing (and still are) to go to their death out of allegiance to this Man?

He is risen!
He is risen indeed!
He is risen!
He is risen indeed!
He is risen!
He is risen indeed!

He not only has risen, He is the firstborn from the dead. Colossians 1:18: *"And he (Jesus) is the head of the body, the church; he is the beginning and the firstborn from among the dead, so that in everything he might have supremacy."*

Firstborn from among the dead, wait a minute. There were all kinds of people raised from the dead in the Bible: Both Elijah and Elisha raised someone, there's the daughter of Jairus, the widow of Nain's son and of course Lazarus. How can Jesus be the firstborn from among the dead?

Here's the difference. They all died again! Jesus hasn't and won't. He died, descended into hell. Got the t-shirt and the keys from the devil, and now is alive forevermore. He has unlocked the dominion of death for all who love him. Notice, He is the firstborn, not the only-born from among the dead. There are more to come! Because He conquered death, we can too!

So we have a message to the Muslim soldier who believes he can sacrifice his life for the cause, go straight to heaven and be in the company of 40 virgins.

We have a message to the Hindu student who lives her life managing karma in hope of advancing just one stage in the next life.

We have a message for the Buddhist mother who hopes to lose her identity in the formless great beyond like a drop of water in the ocean.

We have a message for the secular humanist businessman who believes *"ashes to ashes, dust to dust."* Period. It is over when it is over.

We have a message for the new age university professor who believes that when we die we are in the sun, in the wind and in the rain.

And we have a message for crazy American Christians who still don't get it. You don't need to put trinkets into the coffin of your loved ones. They won't need their false teeth or spare glasses. I read that one grieving widow put two cans of the spray adhesive that her husband needed to secure his toupee into his coffin before his cremation. . .

Did you read that? *Cans of adhesive spray. . .Before his cremation. . .*

Apparently, the explosion bent the furnace door!

We have a message and it is important for us to hit the bulls-eye of that message. Here again are some words by N.T. Wright:

> *"Despite a thousand Easter Hymns and a million Easter sermons, the resurrection narratives in the gospels never, ever say anything like, 'Jesus is raised therefore there is life after death,' let alone, 'Jesus is raised therefore we shall go to heaven when we die.' Not even, in a more authentic first-century Christian way, do they say, 'Jesus is raised, therefore we shall be raised from the dead after the sleep of death.' No. Insofar as the event is interpreted, Easter has a very this-worldly, present age meaning: Jesus is raised, so he is the Messiah, and therefore he is the world's true Lord; Jesus is raised so God's new creation has begun—and we, his followers, have a job to do! Jesus is raised, so we must act as his heralds, announcing his lordship to the entire world, making his kingdom come on earth as in heaven."*

If we get the message right, we will get the right outcome. Look at the change in the lives of Christ's followers after the 40 days between Christ's resurrection and His ascension.

> *"While he was blessing them,*
> *he left them and was taken up into heaven.*
> *Then they worshipped him and*
> *returned to Jerusalem with great joy.*
> *And they stayed continually at the temple,*
> *praising God."* Luke 24:51-53

The 40 days began with confusion, offense, doubt and despair. But it ended with worship, joy and praise. It ended with **altogether LIFE**! This is what the resurrection of Jesus can do for you.

Bible Study

As you study the following passages, keep your pen handy. Ask the Lord to speak to you while you read. Think about how the Lord wants to minister to you, and then think about how He wants to minister through you. Be creative. Write a song based on the scripture. Be a SMART Bible reader. (See Appendix)

> **Matthew 28**
> **Mark 16**
> **Luke 24**
> **Acts 1**

Vintage Poetry – "One Day"

One day when heaven was filled with His praises,
One day when sin was as black as could be,
Jesus came forth to be born of a virgin—
Dwelt amongst men, my example is He!

(chorus)
Living He loved me; dying He saved me;
Buried He carried my sins far away!
Rising He justified freely forever;
One day He's coming—Oh, glorious day!

One day they led Him up Calvary's mountain,
One day they nailed Him to die on the tree;
Suffering anguish, despised and rejected;
Bearing our sins, my Redeemer is He!

One day they left Him alone in the garden,
One day He rested from suffering free;
Angels came down o'er His tomb to keep vigil;
Hope of the hopeless, my Savior is He!

One day the grave could conceal Him no longer,
One day the stone rolled away from the door;
Then He arose, over death He had conquered;
Now is ascended, my Lord evermore!

One day the trumpet will sound for His coming,
One day the skies with His glories will shine;
Wonderful day, my beloved ones bringing;
Glorious Savior, this Jesus is mine!

(chorus)
Living He loved me; dying He saved me;
Buried He carried my sins far away!
Rising He justified freely forever;
One day He's coming—Oh, glorious day!

J. Wilbur Chapman -- 1908

Creative Space

_____

_____

_____

_____

_____

_____

_____

_____

_____

_____

_____

_____

Chapter Two: Heart for the Hopeless

Before we look at Jesus Christ's encounter with Mary Magdalene in John 20, I want to look at a short Bible study from Psalm 46.   The theme of the Psalm is clear in the first verse: *"God is our refuge and strength, an ever present help in trouble."*

The core of the Psalm goes on to describe catastrophe and chaos. There are illusions to earthquakes, floods or possibly tsunamis, even volcanoes. The Psalmist speaks of nations that are in political uproar and war. In the middle and at the end of this Psalm there are two identical verses (7 & 11). Both of them are followed by a mysterious Hebrew word, *Selah*. Most Bible scholars agree that this was probably a sign for a musical interlude. Remember this Psalm was written as a song. It is almost certain that this word *Selah* was at least a call for those hearing the message to stop and meditate on the truth just presented.

Here is the verse repeated twice: *"The Lord Almighty is with us; the God of Jacob is our fortress."*

Why don't you put some music on and meditate on that truth for a while. Have yourself a *Selah*.

Back already? OK, let's break it down. *Lord Almighty*, that can also be translated *Lord of hosts*. That means that God is commander over armies and armies of warring angels. Good news. . .He is with us!

Remember this Old Testament illustration? In 2 Kings 6, we find the King of Aram at war with Israel. Elisha, the prophet of God had an inside track with the Lord Almighty. God was telling Elisha the wicked king's plans. The king of Aram sent a strong force of men, horses and chariots to kill Elisha.

When Elisha's servant looked out of the window, he saw the armies of the enemy surrounding them. He was terrified. Elisha told him not to be afraid and then prayed: *"O Lord, open his eyes so he may see."* The Lord allowed the servant to see that the hills surrounding the enemy were filled with warring angels, horses and chariots of fire from heaven! When the enemy advanced against Elisha, they were struck with blindness from God.

That same Lord of hosts is with us! The God of Jacob is our fortress.

We have some biblical imagery for the word fortress. It revolves around the Hebrew word *Masada*. Herod the Great built a fortress called Masada. It was a mountain with the top cut off of it in southern Israel. On one side there was a 1,300 foot cliff and on the other the Dead Sea. Masada seemed impenetrable. This fortress was necessary for Herod to keep him safe from a Jewish insurrection or an attack by Cleopatra and her Egyptian troops.

The God of Jacob is our Masada, our fortress.

Now wait. . .wouldn't it seem better to switch those sentences around? *The Lord Almighty is our fortress; the God of Jacob is with us.* The One who is commander of armies and armies of angels is our fortress. He will keep us safe. The God of the individual (Jacob) is with us. Doesn't that seem to fit better?

No, let's not switch it. This is our safety, this is our refuge: we have a God who cares about every individual.

> *"The Lord is close to the brokenhearted and saves those who are crushed in spirit."* Psalm 34:18

> *"The Spirit of the Sovereign Lord is on me, because the Lord as anointed me to preach good news to the poor. He has sent me to bind up the broken hearted, to proclaim freedom for the captives and release from darkness for the prisoners, to proclaim the year of the Lord's favor and the day of vengeance of our God, to comfort all who mourn, and provide for those who grieve in Zion—to bestow on them a crown of beauty instead of ashes, the oil of gladness instead of mourning, and a garment of praise instead of a spirit of despair. They will be called oaks of righteousness, a planting of the Lord for the display of his splendor."* Isaiah 61:1-3

The God who focuses on the one, the Good Shepherd Himself, He is our fortress! Now let me illustrate this truth with Christ's encounter with Mary Magdalene in John 20. Read verses 10 through 18.

The outline of this passage is very simple:
1). Mary's crying.
2). Jesus cares.

Mary's crying. Why? She is confused. The last week has been a whirlwind. It began with a triumphal entry into Jerusalem with the whole crowd singing Christ's praises. It ended with the sound of metal hitting metal as the nails were hammered through Jesus into the cross.

And now His body is gone. Did the guards take Him and throw His body into the garbage heap for the dogs? Did they want one more chance to humiliate those who followed Him by stealing and desecrating His body?

Mary is crying because she is sad. That word doesn't seem strong enough. Jesus had freed her from the bondage of seven demons (Luke 8:2). More than that, He had filled her with love and hope and life. Now He is gone, really gone. She is desperate, and even willing to go find the body so that she can bring Him back to His tomb.

Jesus cares. I believe that Christ's appearance to Mary Magdalene was Plan B. Her tears prompted this encounter. Plan A was described in the first 8 verses of Luke 24. This is the plan that was agreed upon in a Holy huddle with Jesus and some angels. The angels would go to the tomb, roll the stone away and wait there for those who loved Christ. When they arrived, they would tell them that Jesus was alive and that He was going to meet with them later. Sounds like a good plan, right?

But Mary was crying. Jesus Cares. So He appeared, it was Plan B. After all, she was right there with Him when He suffered on the cross. In fact, He is intent to fulfill the very prophecy that He gave those who followed Him before His death:

> *"In a little while you will see me no more, and then after a little while you will see me. I tell you the truth, you will weep and mourn while the*

21

world rejoices. You will grieve, but your grief will turn to joy." John 16:19,20

Mary saw Jesus, but though that it must be the gardener. But she realized that it was Jesus when He simply said, *"Mary."* She heard Him say her name and suddenly it now all made sense. He was alive and her grief was transformed into joy.

Isn't it wonderful that Jesus appeared to Mary? The first person that draws the presence of the Risen Lord is a formerly demon possessed woman who is crying. If I were Jesus, I would have made a more powerful first appearance. Maybe to Pilate as he is washing his hands! Tradition says that this man who literally tried to wash his hands from the responsibility of having Jesus crucified lived the rest of his life obsessively washing his hands. I would have just leaned in behind him and non-chalantly said: *"Did you miss a spot?"* Having the resurrected Lord sneak up on him surely would have made Pilate's knees buckle!

But Jesus came to Mary, and His message to her? *"I am returning to my Father and your Father, to my God and your God."* John 20:17 Isn't that beautiful? Jesus appears to a woman who is crying because He cares and then He draws her right in to the intimacy that He has with His Father.

"The Lord Almighty is with us. The God of Mary is our fortress."

If you are confused, if you are sad, if you are grieving, this same Jesus is alive and He still cares. The God of the individual, the Good Shepherd Himself, is with you. And He is your refuge, He is your strength, He is your fortress.

Selah!

Bible Study

In Luke 11:13, Jesus says that if earthly fathers know how to give good gifts to their children, how much more will the Heavenly Father give His Holy Spirit to His children who ask! As you study the following scriptures, believe that the Holy Spirit will give you wildly creative gifts to share with your mentor or your friends. And be SMART (Don't forget about the appendix)!

Psalm 34, 46
Isaiah 61
John 14-16
John 20

Vintage Poetry – "Near to the Heart of God"

There is a place of quiet rest, near to the heart of God.
A place where sin cannot molest, near to the heart of God.
O Jesus blest Redeemer, sent from the heart of God,
Hold us who wait before Thee, near to the heart of God.

There is a place of comfort sweet, near to the heart of God.
A place where we our Savior meet, near to the heart of God.
O Jesus blest Redeemer, sent from the heart of God,
Hold us who wait before Thee, near to the heart of God.

There is a place of full release, near to the heart of God.
A place where all is joy and peace, near to the heart of God.
O Jesus blest Redeemer, sent from the heart of God,
Hold us who wait before Thee, near to the heart of God.

C.B. McAfee – 1903

Creative Space

Chapter Three: Searching the Scriptures

We are walking with Jesus from the day of His resurrection to the day of His ascension: The 40 days of Easter. We are pioneering a new movement, giving Easter the emphasis that it deserves. I've got the first verse to our theme song (to the tune of *"12 Days of Christmas"*):

> *On the first day of Easter,*
> *My true love gave to me,*
> *A tomb that's forever empty!*

39 more verses to go, and you have to repeat each verse with each new one. It's going to be a long song. Could kill the movement. Nevermind.

In this chapter, we are going to look at Luke 24:13-35. It's the story of two guys who were on the wrong road. Go ahead and read it now.

These men were on the road to Emmaus. It was a town about 7 miles northwest of Jerusalem. For these men, it was a road of discussion. They were rehearsing over and over again the events of the last week. How could it have come to this? How could Jesus have been executed like He was? How could all of their dreams have vanished so quickly? This road of discussion became a road of disappointment.

But what were they thinking heading down that road? That very day, they had heard rumors that Jesus had risen. Why in the world would they be leaving Jerusalem now? On the day when Mary Magdalene was seeking Jesus, willing to get His body herself if she had to. These guys were leaving town.

They were on the wrong road.

All of a sudden Jesus just shows up; but they do not recognize Him. He asks them what they are talking about. One of the guys, Cleopas, gets a little sarcastic: *"Did you just drop on to this planet? Are you the only one on this green earth who doesn't know what is happening? Get a newspaper fella!"* (My paraphrase)

Jesus probes deeper. So the men proceed to tell Jesus about His own life. When they finish, Jesus challenges them. I'll use the real text this time:

> *"How foolish you are, and how slow of heart to believe all that the prophets have spoken! Did not the Christ have to suffer these things and then enter his glory?"* Luke 24:25,26

It is really important to see where Jesus' challenge is aimed. It is not aimed at their unwillingness to believe the women's report of His resurrection. His challenge is aimed at their inability to apply scripture to their present circumstance.

They had sluggish hearts, and their faith was short-sighted. But here is the good news: Jesus challenged them as their **companion** on their journey! He's got 40 days before He ascends to the Father, and these guys on the wrong road are on His heart! Amazing. . .

Who are these guys anyway? Cleopas? The other guy isn't even named. They sure don't sound like leads in the storyline. With Jesus, there is no supporting cast, we are all leads in His story. He is the Good Shepherd. The God of Jacob, an individual. He is our fortress!

Selah.

What Jesus does next makes me green with envy. While walking with them to Emmaus, He searches the scriptures with them. The Word Himself, takes them on an Old Testament survey! And He shows them all that the Old Testament scriptures say about Him!

Jesus is Noah's ark of safety in a world flooded with sin.
He's Abraham's once and for all sacrifice.
He is the fulfillment of Moses' law.

Jesus is David's dance partner,
Solomon's wisdom and Isaiah's Emmanuel.
He is Jeremiah's branch,
Daniel's stone not cut with hands,
Hosea's lily and Joel's hope.

Jesus is Amos' plowman overtaking the reaper.
He's Jonah's sign, Nahum's peace
and Obadiah's deliverance.

Jesus is Habakkuk's song of salvation,
He is Zechariah's holiness unto the Lord.
And He is both Malachi's refiner's fire
and sun of righteousness!

Jesus is at the very center of one storyline from God that began in Genesis chapter one. God, the Father, is reconciling His world as well as the people He created in His image!

The guys on the wrong road will later report that as Jesus was teaching them, their hearts were burning. That's the same thing that happened to John Wesley, the founder of the Methodist revival and church planting movement. He was an Anglican priest and former failed missionary to America. He attended a meeting where someone was reading Martin Luther's preface to the book of Romans. In His words: *"I felt my heart strangely warmed."* I believe that was Wesley's conversion to Christ. He encountered the Risen Lord.

When our travelers reached their destination, Jesus acted as if He were going on. In good Middle Eastern hospitality, they urged Him to spend the night with them and invited Him to have a meal. Remember, they still do not know that this is Jesus.

> *"When He was at the table with them, he took bread, gave thanks, broke it and began to give it to them. Then their eyes were opened and they recognized him, and he disappeared from their sight."* Luke 24:30,31

What opened their eyes to the reality of Christ's presence? Maybe it was the similarity their meal had to Christ's last supper? Maybe when Jesus handed them the bread it was the first time that they could see His hands with the nail scars?

I think that their eyes were opened when Jesus moved from their guest to their host.

What road are you on?

How well have you applied the Bible to your life?

How long has it been since your heart burned?

Is Jesus your guest, or is He your host?

Bible Study

As you read some Old Testament passages in preparation for your time one on one or in a small group, be SMART (appendix). Look for Jesus in these passages and wait for Jesus to make Himself known to you.

Genesis 1-3
Psalm 22, 27
Isaiah 53, 55
Malachi 1-4

Vintage Poetry – "More About Jesus"

More about Jesus would I know,
More of His grace to others show;
More of His saving fullness see,
More of His love who died for me.

(Chorus)
More, more about Jesus,
More, more about Jesus;
More of His saving fullness see,
More of His love who died for me.

More about Jesus let me learn,
More of His holy will discern
Spirit of God, my teacher be,
Showing the things of Christ to me.

More about Jesus on His throne,
Riches in glory all His own;
More of His kingdoms sure increase;
More of His coming, Prince of Peace.

(Chorus)
More, more about Jesus,
More, more about Jesus;
More of His saving fullness see,
More of His love who died for me.

Eliza E. Hewitt – 1887

Creative Space

_____

_____

_____

_____

_____

_____

_____

_____

_____

_____

_____

Chapter Four: Peace through Proof

Any parent that has more than one child probably has experienced this mystery: How can the same two people produce such different children? We have four and they are all very different.

Each of them responded to discipline differently. I'll go down from the oldest. Zachary is the prototype firstborn. When he did something wrong, he usually took responsibility and realized that he missed the standard. Jacob was just always happy, even in discipline. It's really hard to discipline a happy child! Jessica could be disciplined with just a look. When Corrie Emma was being disciplined, she could give you a look that made you think that you were the one who had done something wrong!

In this chapter, we are going to look at the same encounter that Jesus had with the disciples from three different gospels. It's amazing to see the varying perspectives. After reading each passage, we will see two of the main reasons that Jesus appeared over the 40 Days of Easter:

    1). To offer peace
    2). To give proof

Read Mark 16:14.

Wow. That sounds pretty intense! It's just one verse and the crux of it is a rebuke from Jesus for the disciples' stubborn refusal to believe. Mark's Gospel comes from his interaction with Peter. This is Peter's perspective of the encounter. I wonder how much of his perspective is colored by the shame he felt after his denial of Jesus?

Read Luke 24:36-45

This is not so intense. In this account, we see that Christ's primary message is "peace." And it seems the primary means to peace is proof. Jesus goes to great lengths to prove to His disciples that He is alive. Jesus invites His friends to look at Him and even touch Him:

"Touch me and see, a ghost does not have flesh and bones as you see I have."

Just when their minds were spinning with "too good to be true delight," Jesus asks if they had any food. He takes some broiled fish and eats right in front of them! He will prove that He is alive and that He has a real resurrected body!

Is it any wonder that John (one of the disciples in the room) would later write in his 1st epistle: *"That which was from the beginning, which we have heard, which we have seen with our eyes, which we have looked at and our hands have touched —this we proclaim concerning the Word of life."* I John 1:1

Jesus wanted them to have peace, so He gave them convincing proof that He was alive. In verse 45, Jesus roots their experience in scripture. He opened their minds so that they could understand. How amazing it must have been to sit with the resurrected Lord and have Him weave the thread of truth concerning the resurrection from the Old Testament in their midst!

Read John 20:19-23

In John's account, we get the little tidbit that the disciples were in a room with locked doors because of their fear of the Jews. The inference from this is that Christ's resurrected body is not hindered by locked doors. He suddenly is standing among them. His message?

"Peace be with you!"

As soon as He greets them, He begins showing them His scars. This is a sign of Christ's common humanity with the rest of us. What is it about men in particular that makes us want to show off our scars? I have been in countless hospital rooms as a pastor and have seen way too many scars!

After the disciples see Christ's hands and feet, He offers them more peace: Jesus said, *"Peace be with you!"* They must have needed it!

In verse 22, Jesus breathed on them and said, *"Receive the Holy Spirit."* Christ's heart for these men is that they have peace instead of fear and proof so that they will not be troubled. In Luke's gospel, He opens their mind so that they will understand the plan of God according to the scripture. Now, in John's account, they receive divine help that will go directly to their heart. Jesus gives them the Holy Spirit. The Spirit will come alongside them and guide them into truth.

We've looked at one encounter between Jesus and His disciples in three different gospels. Why did Jesus do these things? Yes, He wanted them to have peace. Yes, they needed to have hands on proof to have this peace. But what is at the heart of Jesus actions?

He wanted them to believe and to believe deeply. He appealed to their eyes by letting them see and touch Him. He appealed to their minds so that they would understand the storyline of God from the Old to the New Testaments. And He appealed to their hearts by giving them the Holy Spirit.

All of us develop faith through each of these three levels: eyes, mind and heart. And each of these levels have sight connected to them. Obviously, we can see with our eyes. But we also see with our minds. In fact, when your mind comes to a new understanding we often describe that by saying, *"I see!"*

The strongest of all sight is in our heart (our emotion). Have you heard the phrase: *"Love is blind?"* When we see with our heart, it has power to overrule both our mind and our eyes.

Jesus appealed to three levels of sight in this encounter with the disciples: eyes, mind and heart. He knew that these men would be willing to engage in belief in all three levels. Jesus didn't appear to Pilate or Caiaphas or even Caesar. He could engage their eyes and even their mind, but they would not have engaged their heart in belief in Jesus.

"The Christ would build His Church not upon wonder or astonishment or fear. He would build His Church upon nothing but love."
Doremus A. Hayes

I preached a series of services in a campmeeting in central PA where they had 15 people who were called Camp VIP's – Visually Impaired People. These men and women were completely blind. They were a delight to preach to, very involved in the message. Almost all of them would talk back to me as I was preaching.

At the end of a message on believing Jesus at the heart level instead of just the eyes or mind, I gave them a test. I asked them the following questions:

1). If I could give you your eyesight tonight, would you be willing to give me your ability to understand? In other words, you get to see, but you also would function as though you had Alzheimer's disease.

Several of them responded with a polite *"No thank you."*

2). If I could give you your eyesight tonight, would you be willing to give away your ability to give and receive love?

This got a rousing response: *"Not a chance, one man said!"*

3). If I could give you your eyesight tonight, would you be willing to give up ever encountering Jesus' love and power again?

This time they were indignant: *"Absolutely not! No way!"*

It turns out, they may have been the least impaired people in the meeting! They could see Jesus with their minds and their hearts and they would not trade that for a lesser sight.

What about you? Jesus has made Himself known. He is alive and real.

How have your responded? What level of belief do you have? He expects more than a surface belief or a mental assent. He will offer peace and proof so that he can fully engage your heart of faith.

Bible Study

With some SMART study, read these chapters and jot down insight that the Lord gives you. Let yourself be creative and write some thoughts down to share with friends.

I John 1
I John 2
I John 3
I John 4
I John 5

Vintage Poetry

This great hymn was written by Fanny Crosby. She was blinded by a doctor's error when she was a little girl. But notice how well she sees through her heart in verse two and three!

Blessed assurance, Jesus is mine!
Oh, what a foretaste of glory divine!
Heir of salvation, purchase of God,
Born of His Spirit, washed in His blood.

> (Chorus)
> This is my story, this is my song,
> Praising my Savior all the day long;

This is my story, this is my song,
Praising my Savior all the day long.

Perfect submission, perfect delight,
Visions of rapture now burst on my sight;
Angels, descending, bring from above
Echoes of mercy, whispers of love.

Perfect submission, all is at rest,
I in my Savior am happy and blest,
Watching and waiting, looking above,
Filled with His goodness, lost in His love.

Fanny Crosby – 1873

Creative Space

_____

_____

_____

_____

_____

_____

_____

_____

_____

_____

_____

_____

Chapter Five: Dispelling the Doubt

There's no doubt about it, Thomas has gotten a bad rap! How would you like to be tagged for 2000 years with your moment of greatest weakness? I have battled with the sin of anger, and I am really glad that people do not refer to me as "angry Rich!"

We don't do that with other folks from the Bible. . . Drunken Noah, Lying Abraham, Murdering Moses, Adulterating (I think I just made a word up) David.

Why do we need to immortalize Thomas with this description: Doubting Thomas?

Let's look at the story: Read John 20:24-31

This is the 2nd encounter that the disciples had with the resurrected Lord. And Thomas missed the 1st one. That's big.

Thomas is on the outside looking in at the rest of the disciples. Have you ever been the one person within your group of friends who missed the great event? Thomas missed the first encounter with Jesus. He missed Jesus opening the minds of the disciples and he missed the Holy Spirit being breathed upon him. All Thomas had were the words of his friends. No wonder Thomas is struggling!

Jesus appears again, and this time Thomas is right in the center of it all. I love to picture the scene that we just looked at in John 20. . .

I see Thomas holding court in the middle of the disciples. Listen to him: *If I said it once, I'll say it again. I will not believe this resurrection story unless I see Him myself; unless I see the nail scars and inspect the wound, I just won't . . .*

Thomas stops in mid-sentence because all attention in the room is away from him and there is not a sound coming from any of the disciples. All eyes are big and focused on the same thing. Thomas becomes aware that someone else is in the room. He says: *He's here, isn't He. He's behind me, isn't He.* The disciples slowly shake their head yes.

I don't know if it happened like that, but we do know that Jesus just appeared in their midst even though the doors were locked because of their fear. Christ's resurrection body is flesh and blood, but it is not like ours!

Can you imagine what was going on in Thomas' analytical mind?

Jesus leads with His important greeting: *Peace be with you!"* Then He zeros right in on Thomas: *Put your finger here; see my hands. Reach out your hand and put it into my side. Stop doubting and believe.*

Let's take a rabbit trail for a few minutes with this question: **Is doubting the same as unbelief?**

41

Roget's Thesaurus lists the antonym for doubt as belief. So there must be a connection. But Jesus confronts some ugly unbelief in His ministry and the way that He does it looks a whole lot different than the way He engages Thomas.

Read John 8:42-47.

Now there is some ugly unbelief! And Jesus doesn't mince any words with them. He tells them that they are children of the devil!

There must be a difference between a doubting disciple and an obstinate unbeliever.

Back to the story. When Jesus engages Thomas and offers to let him inspect His wounds, Thomas loses his analytical edge. He doesn't circle around Jesus, rub his chin and respond dryly: *Well, I have deduced through the empirical evidence that you are in fact you and you are in fact alive.*

Thomas cries out from his heart: *My Lord and my God!* That sounds like worship! In fact, this is the highest statement of faith recorded in the gospels! No doubt about it, Thomas got a bad rap!

Do you doubt?

Don't just go right to the next sentence in this chapter. Go back to that question and wrestle a little with it. I'm guessing that if you are this far into this study, you are not an obstinate unbeliever. But you may be a doubting disciple.

Jesus' word to you is: *Stop doubting and believe.*

Here's a little test that will help you navigate through your doubt and into belief. It centers on three words: Future, Fruit and Fight.

Future

"Against all hope, Abraham in hope believed and so became the father of many nations, just as it had been said to him, 'So shall your offspring be.' Without weakening in his faith, he faced the fact that his body was as good as dead – since he was about a hundred years old – and that Sarah's womb was also dead. Yet he did not waver through unbelief regarding the promise of God, but was strengthened in his faith and gave glory to God being fully persuaded that God had power to do what he had promised." Romans 4:18-21

Test Question #1: What do you believe about your future?

Fruit

". . . By faith we eagerly await through the Spirit the righteousness for which we hope. For in Christ Jesus neither circumcision (focusing on the law) nor uncircumcision (focusing on your freedom) has any value. The only thing that counts is faith expressing itself through love." Galatians 5:5,6

Test Question #2: Do people like being around you?

Fight

"For I am already being poured out like a drink offering, and the time has come for my departure. I have fought the good fight, I have finished the race, I have kept the faith. Now there is in store for me the crown of righteousness, which the Lord, the righteous judge, will award to me on that day – and not only to me, but also to all who have longed for his appearing." 2 Timothy 4:6-8

43

Test Question #3: Are you still in the fight?

As you wrestle with those questions, I believe that the Holy Spirit will talk to you. Take a couple of days and keep going back to both the scriptures and the questions. Stay alert and keep a record of what the Spirit is saying about doubt and belief in your life.

In closing, I want to show you how well the Apostle Paul did on a test of doubt and belief. Go back to 2 Timothy 4:9-22. Paul is closing his letter to his young friend, Timothy. Paul writes as an elder apostle who bears on his body the marks of following Christ. He is old, he is alone, he is under arrest and he is awaiting his execution. But he is confident in his future, growing the fruit of love and still in the fight.

Here are some bullet points in these final paragraphs:

v. 9 – Paul urges Timothy to get to him quickly
v. 10 – Demas has deserted him
v. 13 – Paul needs his coat and his scrolls and parchments
v. 14 – Alexander opposed the message and harmed Paul
v. 16 – The church didn't defend Paul, the Lord stood with him
v. 17 – Paul was delivered from the lion's mouth
v. 21 – Paul urges Timothy to get there before winter

Go over that list again. Did you see it?

Let me give you some context. Paul served as the great missionary of the Bible. He faithfully served Christ's Kingdom purposes among the Gentiles. He would eventually give his life for Christ. This letter is written near the very end of Paul's life. He's old, alone, in prison and he is cold.

v. 13 – Paul asks Timothy to be sure to bring his coat

v. 21 – He says to Timothy: *"Do your best to get here before winter."*

In the midst of such suffering, this letter ends with a blessing: *The Lord be with your spirit. Grace be with you.*

Paul believed: His future was secure, his fruit ripe until the end and he never gave up the fight.

You can access the same power that dispels doubt.

Bible Study

With some SMART study, read these chapters and jot down insight that the Lord gives you.

John 8
Romans 4
Galatians 5
2 Timothy 4

Vintage Poetry – "Be Still My Soul"

Be still, my soul: the Lord is on thy side;
Bear patiently the cross of grief or pain;
Leave to thy God to order and provide;
In ev'ry change he faithful will remain.
Be still, my soul: thy best, thy heav'nly friend
Through thorny ways leads to a joyful end.

Be still, my soul: thy God doth undertake
To guide the future as he has the past.
Thy hope, thy confidence let nothing shake;
All now mysterious shall be bright at last.

Be still, my soul: the waves and winds still know
His voice who ruled them while he dwelt below.

Be still, my soul: when dearest friends depart,
And all is darkened in the vale of tears,
Then shalt thou better know his love, his heart,
Who comes to soothe thy sorrow and thy fears.
Be still, my soul: thy Jesus can repay
From his own fullness all he takes away.

Be still, my soul: the hour is hast'ning on
When we shall be forever with the Lord,
When disappointment, grief, and fear are gone,
Sorrow forgot, love's purest joys restored.
Be still, my soul: when change and tears are past,
All safe and blessed we shall meet at last.

Katharina von Schlegel – 1752

Creative Space

_____

_____

_____

_____

_____

_____

_____

_____

_____

_____

_____

_____

Chapter Six: Road to Restoration

40 days of Easter. . .we are looking at the days that followed the resurrection and led up to Christ's ascension. We are getting a close-up view of what was on the heart of Jesus before He ascended to His throne at the right hand of His Father. He had just 40 days, so He :

Comforted a crying woman
Went after a couple of nobodies on the wrong road
Gave shalom to some fearful disciples
Proved that He was alive again and again
Caused a doubting disciple to worship

These activities are still on His heart. Maybe He is engaging you in this study in some of the same ways.

In this chapter, we are going to see Jesus at His best while Peter is at his worst. Jesus will reveal His full power of restoration when a friend falls. And Peter will never be the same.

We will journey on Peter's road to restoration. As we walk with Peter and Jesus, there are six stops to make on the road. Get your bible and let's travel together. *You* may never be the same.

Jesus is at His best. In these hours before Peter denies even knowing Him, Jesus is lovingly preparing Peter for the worst night of his life. I am struck by the love of Jesus. He begins restoring Peter even before he falls!

Let's look at the first stop on this road to restoration:

Matthew 26:31-35

Through His command of Old Testament scripture, Jesus prepared His disciples for a prophetic fulfillment of an event first given to the prophet Zechariah centuries before Jesus was born: *"Strike the shepherd and the sheep will be scattered. . ."* Zechariah 13:7

Jesus prepared His disciples for what would happen when He was arrested. He warned them that they would run like scattered sheep and they would fall. But look again at the promise He gave them in Matthew 26:32: *"But after I have risen, I will go ahead of you into Galilee."*

Jesus is now hours before his own crucifixion. He will be arrested, beaten, whipped to the very edge of his life, and nailed to a cross. He will literally go to hell and back. And then he will rise from the dead.

Before He leaves on His road, He wants his disciples to know that they have a road to restoration. He tells them that He knows where they will be after they fall and He will go ahead of them and be there. . .waiting.

Have you fallen? Jesus knows where you will be and He goes ahead of you. He waits for you.

Peter is aghast at the thought that he would fall. Watch what he does:

"Even if all fall away. . .I never will."

Can you believe it? He throws the rest of the guys under the bus. He basically says: I can see Your point with these guys, but not me! Peter is so cocky. It's no coincidence that he will share the stage on this night of denial with a rooster!

Jesus is clear. Before the rooster crows tomorrow morning, Peter will disown Jesus three times.

Let's go to the next stop on the road to restoration:

Matthew 26:36-41

Jesus took His three closest friends and went to a garden to pray. He doesn't need their wisdom and He doesn't need their protection. He just needs them to *be* with Him.

Jesus prays and experiences agony. He deals the devil a deathblow when He declares that it's not about what He wants, only what His Father wants.

Three times in this agony He checks on His friends. All three times they are asleep. Christ's question still echoes: *"Could you men not keep watch with me for one hour?"*

I want to focus on one particular phrase that Jesus gave in the midst of His friend's sleepiness: *"The spirit is willing but the body is weak."*

That seems to be the extent of His reprimand. He is sweating drops of blood in agony and His friends are sleeping right through it because of their weak flesh. But did you hear what else He said?

"Your spirit is willing."

Even when they are letting Him down in such a crucial battle of intercession, He lets them know that He knows what is inside of them.

Jesus knows that they have a great big "YES" in their spirit for Him. They love Jesus, and He knows it. In fact, it is this *"willing spirit"* that separates these men from Judas on this dark night.

The third stop on our road is:

Luke 22:31,32

Focus on what is in the mind of Jesus. In these hours of intense personal emotion, Christ's heart is for Peter. Satan has asked to sift Peter like wheat. Like in the days of Job, Satan is sure that he can pull him into the abyss of sin and hopelessness. But Jesus is praying for Peter. Wow.

Remember the Selah? We better take one! Hours before His death, Jesus is not concerned about Himself, He is praying for Peter. I love this man!

Now watch how Jesus prophetically speaks into Peter's restoration: *"When you have turned back, strengthen your brothers."*

That is too good! Before Peter even falls, Jesus is prophetically picturing his return. He's letting him know that He will need Peter's help with the rest of the boys. When it looks like it is over, it won't be over.

Have you been sifted? Has the enemy tried to convince you that it is over? Stay on the road with me. This gets even better.

Stop number four:

Luke 22:54-62

This is Peter at his worst. After Jesus is arrested, Peter follows at a distance. Therein lies part of the problem. He was not willing to be fully identified with Jesus. He stayed in the shadows for fear of his life. On this dark night, John stays beside Jesus and Peter stayed behind Him. It is good for us to recognize that we are very prone to denial when we keep a distance from Jesus.

Peter comes out of the shadows to warm himself by the fire in the courtyard. In the shimmering light, he is recognized.

"You are with Him." A woman declares.

"Not me. I don't know Him." Peter answers.

A little later, someone else interjects: *"You are one of them."*

"You must have me confused with someone else. I'm not with Him!" Peter exclaims.

An hour or so later, someone says with certainty: *"This fellow was with Him, for he is Galilean!"*

Peter summons all of his strength and fully denies his involvement with Jesus. And then the rooster crows. Can you imagine how that sounded to Peter?

By far, there was something worse than the sound of the rooster. A moment after Jesus came out of the courtroom. The Bible says that Jesus looked straight at Peter. The word used to describe how Jesus looked at him is not a glance but a gaze. In fact, it is the same word used to describe how Jesus looked at Peter in their first meeting. Jesus gazed at Simon and immediately changed his name to Peter. He looked deeply within Simon and saw that He was a rock, so Jesus called him that...Peter.

What was in that gaze from Jesus in the courtyard? We know what it caused. . .Peter ran from the courtyard weeping bitterly.

Do you think it was anger? Disappointment? Disgust?

All the other stops up until this point should lead us to believe that there was great love in the gaze. It is who Jesus is.

The fifth stop on Peter's road to restoration is a quick one and it may be my favorite:

Mark 16:7

Jesus is alive. When the women arrive at His tomb to anoint His body, they are shocked to see that the stone is rolled away and the tomb is empty. Looking inside and to the right, they see a young man dressed in white. They are freaked!

He calms their fear and says, *"You are looking for Jesus the Nazarene, who was crucified. He has risen! He is not here. See the place where they laid him."*

What follows is my favorite part: *"Go tell His disciples and Peter, He is going ahead of you into Galilee. There you will see Him, just as He told you."*

Did you see it? Just two words...

"And Peter."

I love those two words! Angels are messengers. They deliver messages, right? You can bet that the angel given the duty of the empty tomb got it right. He delivered the message without error. That means that Jesus gave him those words. It was important to Jesus that the women know that they were to tell the disciples AND PETER! I can hear Jesus reinforcing that message...

"Don't forget to tell them to make sure they tell Peter that I am alive...it's not over. I'm going ahead of him so that I can see him again."

There's something else important about those two words. Jesus uses the name Peter. This is kind of confusing. At the beginning of the gospels, Jesus changes the name of Simon to Peter, which means "rock." But then throughout the gospel story, Jesus always refers to him as Simon. He doesn't use the name Peter. Look back in the gospels for yourself.

But then, after Simon is at his worst, Jesus calls him Peter. Isn't that amazing? Jesus is saying, *"You are still a rock!"*

That ROCKS!!!

The final stop on this road to restoration is

John 21:1-25

Whenever I read this scene, I pretend that I am a director making a movie. I think about what I would have the camera focus on, what the soundtrack would be like. I ask myself tons of questions about what it must have looked like and what was important.

The scene opens with Peter in a familiar place, on the water fishing. Some of the disciples are with him. He has not been fully restored with Jesus yet. They have fished through the night and haven't caught anything. On their way to shore, a figure on the beach shouts to them the question that fishermen must hate, especially when it has been a night without fish:

"Did you catch anything?"

One of the disciples shouts back: *"No."*

The guy on the beach offers an idea: *"Why don't you throw your nets on the other side of the boat?"*

With a we've got nothing to lose attitude, they oblige. The camera zooms in on Peter rolling his eyes. When they pull in the nets they have 152 fish! The camera pulls back from the fish flopping around on the floor of the boat and begins slowly zooming in on the face of John. He is gazing at the figure on the beach. When you get a close up of John's face, he says with authority, *"It's the Lord!"*

Within seconds, while the camera is still on John, you hear a great, big splash! Peter is already in the water. He is swimming to shore to get to Jesus.

It's interesting, he doesn't ask to walk on water this time!

When he gets to the beach you see Jesus at a fire cooking some fish.

What? Where did He get his fish? The disciples, former fishermen, have been out all night with a boat and nets and they didn't catch anything! Jesus is by Himself and He has fish cooking already!

This is how I picture it. He just stood on the shoreline with a frying pan and His index finger. With one motion He commanded the fish to jump into the pan!

Watch this. . .When the boat arrives at the shoreline with 152 fish, Jesus asks: *"Do you guys have any fish? Why don't you bring some of what you have and put it with what I have and we all can have lunch."*

I love this. First, can we agree that all of the fish in this story are from Jesus? He had His fish, God knows how. And He miraculously allowed the fishless fishermen to catch some fish. They were all because of Jesus. Then He uses what they had with what He has so that they can fellowship together around a meal.

This is perfect imagery regarding what our ministry looks like. Everything we have is from Jesus, all our gifts, wisdom, etc. But He asks us to bring what we have and put it with what He has. It goes like this:

"Moses, what's that in your hand?" God asks.

Moses answers, *"A Rod."*

"Perfect!" God exclaims. *"Let's go get Pharaoh!"*

"David, what do you have? God inquires.

David answers, *"A sling and some stones."*

"Excellent, let's go get the giant!"
You get the idea. Jesus let them bring some fish to the table with His fish and they all got to fellowship around a meal. He will do the same for you in ministry.

After breakfast, Jesus invites Peter to take a walk with Him. It must have been a slow, thoughtful walk. I see Peter reserved, with his head down as he politely engages in conversation with Jesus. Finally, Jesus cuts to the chase with a penetrating question:

"Simon, son of John, do you love me?"

Peter answers truthfully, *"You know that I love you."*

Three times Jesus asks this question. And with each answer, Peter's head rises higher and his voices echoes more clearly.

"You know all things, you know that I love you!"

Jesus gives Peter the chance to counter each of the three denials. And with each response, Peter receives reconciliation. Denial is absorbed in a declaration of love. And three times, Jesus is able to direct Peter's future ministry as a shepherd in Christ's Church.

What follows the full reconciliation is astounding. Jesus gives Peter a prophetic word about how he would die and challenges Peter with one mandate.

Jesus uses this phrase in His prophetic word to Peter regarding his old age: *"They will stretch out your hands."*

Apparently, this Greek phrase could not be interpreted in any other way but crucifixion. John gives the commentary that Jesus was indicating the kind of death Peter would experience.

I am amazed at the faith of Peter. Jesus trusted him with the knowledge of his own cruel martyrdom. And

Peter remained faithful. For decades, Peter knew what was coming. And he remained faithful.

That is the power of full reconciliation!

Christ also simplified Peter's ministry with one mandate: *"Follow me."*

It did not have to be more intricate than that, simply follow Jesus.

I love that Peter remains Peter even after reconciliation. He turns and sees John following he and Jesus and asks: *"What about him?"*

Jesus answers: *"That's none of your business!"* And then reiterates the simple mandate: *"You must follow me."*

Well there it is. The end of Peter's road to restoration. It wasn't over after Peter's fall. And Peter was a rock! In fact, according to Church history, Peter was to be crucified exactly like Jesus. But in a last request, he asked for his cross to be turned upside down because he was not worthy to die like His Lord. Wow. There is power in Christ's restoration!

If you have denied Jesus in any way, are you on the road to restoration?

Bible Study

Study SMART!
   Matthew 26
   Luke 22
   Mark 16
   John 21

Vintage Poetry – "Come Thou Fount"

Come, Thou Fount of every blessing,
Tune my heart to sing Thy grace;
Streams of mercy, never ceasing,
Call for songs of loudest praise.
Teach me some melodious sonnet,
Sung by flaming tongues above.
Praise the mount! I'm fixed upon it,
Mount of Thy redeeming love.

Sorrowing I shall be in spirit,
Till released from flesh and sin,
Yet from what I do inherit,
Here Thy praises I'll begin;
Here I raise my Ebenezer;
Here by Thy great help I've come;
And I hope, by Thy good pleasure,
Safely to arrive at home.

Jesus sought me when a stranger,
Wandering from the fold of God;
He, to rescue me from danger,
Interposed His precious blood;
How His kindness yet pursues me
Mortal tongue can never tell,
Clothed in flesh, till death shall loose me
I cannot proclaim it well.

O to grace how great a debtor
Daily I'm constrained to be!
Let Thy goodness, like a fetter,
Bind my wandering heart to Thee.
Prone to wander, Lord, I feel it,
Prone to leave the God I love;
Here's my heart, O take and seal it,
Seal it for Thy courts above.

O that day when freed from sinning,
I shall see Thy lovely face;
Clothed then in blood washed linen
How I'll sing Thy sovereign grace;
Come, my Lord, no longer tarry,
Take my ransomed soul away;
Send thine angels now to carry
Me to realms of endless day.

Robert Robinson – 1758

Creative Space

_____

_____

_____

_____

_____

_____

_____

_____

_____

_____

_____

Chapter Seven: Command and Commission

Do you remember C. S. Lewis' famous argument regarding who Jesus really is? After giving great detail on what Jesus said about Himself, Lewis' logic was impeccable:

"He is either a liar, a lunatic, or He is Lord."

Certainly one of the statements that Lewis was referring to is Matthew 28:16-20. Take a look at this highly charged passage.

Jesus is in Command

Before Jesus ascends into heaven, He gathers the faithful around Him and declares this truth: *"All authority in heaven and earth has been given to me."*

If Jesus is not a liar or a lunatic, then based on this passage He is absolutely in command. And this verse is in the present tense. He will not gain authority at some future event. He is not in some holding pattern waiting for His time. He isn't backstage waiting for a curtain to rise. He doesn't have His fingers crossed hoping that He gets power. He is King, and He is King right now.

His rule and His authority will not come when He returns. He had all the power and all the authority there is in Matthew 28, and He still has it now. Right now, He is seated on a throne far above all evil power. He is not twiddling his thumbs nor is He wringing His hands. Right now, He is orchestrating the events of the end of this age to perfectly fulfill His purposes on this earth.

King Jesus has all authority over creation; He causes the sun to rise each morning. He has all authority over nations; He sets rulers in their place. And He has all authority over you and me. He is just as able to use Billy Graham to fulfill His purposes as He is Achmadinejad (ruler of Iran). Remember, God used both Daniel and Nebuchadnezzar. Jesus has a plan and He has never missed a beat. He has all the authority and He is fully in command.

Are you worried about our government and our leaders? Jesus is our King, there is no need for us to be wringing our hands in worry. Our world is not spiraling out of control. As the old song says, *"He's got the whole world in His hands."* Even the *"tiny little baby!"*

While it seems that the Middle East is up for grabs, we know a different story. Israel will survive as God's people and ultimately every rival kingdom will bow before their Messiah. He has all the authority and He is fully in command.

Does your life seem to be spiraling out of control?

I heard a great story about a father and his five year old son. The dad decided to take his boy to the amusement park. When he got there, the father realized why it had been 25 years since he had gone to a park. He couldn't stand to go on rides that went in circles. They would make him sick.

The boy, however, loved them! Especially the Merry-go-round. When he saw the horses, he pleaded with his father, *"Daddy can we ride them?"*

The father couldn't let the boy down. They got on the ride and the young son picked out his favorite color horse. The dad anticipated just standing next to his son, but the operator came around checking and told the father, *"If you are going to be on the ride, you've got o be on a horse."*

So the father saddled up. When the ride started, the dad was disturbed. He not only had a horse that went around and around, but up and down as well!

It only took a few rotations before the father felt his stomach moving upwards. He lost some color in his face. This was not going well.

The operator was a pro. He could tell things were going from bad to worse. He motioned for the father to come into the center where he was. There he could stand right next to his son. The father noticed something about the center of a merry-go-round. Everything was still going round and round and up and down all around him. But standing in the center with the man who was in control, there was peace.

That's where you need to be right now. Standing in the center with Jesus who is in control.

We have been commissioned

The first word of our commission is GO. We have an active faith. Like Jesus, we are not to be backstage waiting for the curtain to rise. We were never meant to just huddle behind stained glass windows. Those who love Jesus were meant to be moving with such force that even the gates of hell would not be able to stand against our march.

When you received Christ, you did not enter a mansion so that Jesus could be your butler. You enlisted. And if you are not on active duty right now, you should consider these possibilities: either you were never saved or you have gone AWOL!

Where do we go? INTO ALL THE WORLD. Really? Do we all need passports? Probably not. But each one of us should have a world perspective on Christianity. We all need to own the commission into all nations. There ought to be some tangible evidence in our lives that we are committed to this. We can pray, give and go.

As we GO, we MAKE DISCIPLES. Our goal is to reproduce fully devoted followers of Jesus. We not only share our faith, but we work to get new believers firmly rooted in faith.

One of my heroes in the faith is John Wesley. Early in my ministry, I read through volumes of his journals. One entry changed my life. It has served as a compass for me in ministry time and time again. I will paraphrase his words:

"I am convinced that the devil wants nothing more than this, for me to half awaken a people and leave them to their slumber. I will not strike one blow where I can not follow that blow."

Therein lies the genius of the Wesleyan movement. John wasn't satisfied with preaching in the fields to thousands of people. He established the class meeting. New believers would meet regularly with established believers and these classes would focus on discipleship.

This is the purpose of the **altogether LIFE** series. It's why I've chosen to write in this book and the volumes that will follow. I am believing for a holy virus that spreads discipleship in all the world!

What do we do with new disciples? We BAPTIZE them in the name of the Father, Son and Spirit. Why do we baptize? Mostly because Jesus said so, and remember, He has all the authority in heaven and on earth. But there is more. Baptism becomes an opportunity for the new believer to declare his or her faith publically. Baptism is a means of grace. It's a chance for the Holy Spirit to come to the new believer with greater power and intensity.

The most beautiful thing about baptism is the family dynamic. It is never meant to be in isolation. It is a family celebration. Baptism is the entryway into the family room of the church.

In this commission, we are also told to teach. Are we all to become teachers? Yes and no. We won't all function primarily as teachers in God's family. But at some level, I think we all should teach. I believe strongly that we have over professionalized ministry. We look for superstars and then we flock to them in droves. In the establishment of these mega-ministries, I think we have lost something. There is great value in a handful of people sitting around a kitchen table with open bibles. The kitchen table can accommodate even a stuttering voice.

Ultimately, we teach through the counsel of the Holy Spirit, and He is available to the superstar and to you. I've been drawing your attention in each chapter to the appendix that gives details about a SMART Bible Reader. He or she is one who:

Studies
Meditates
Applies
Responds
Teaches

You have been commissioned to look for ways to pass on what Jesus has given to you.

3 Questions

I want to close this chapter with three questions I would like you to think about and discuss with others as you walk out your commission. I will give you an outline to follow.

1). What is our message?

To the world – Reconciliation (God, others, earth)
Repentance (Sorrow and change)
This message is rooted in Christ crucified

To the Church – Holiness (Power over sin)
Hope (Resurrection of our bodies)
This message is rooted in Christ's resurrection

2). What is our Mission?

To know the Word (both the Son and the Scripture)

In John 1, Jesus is called the Word. He is the perfect expression of God. Intimacy with Jesus is our primary mission. You know Him by living in the reality of His presence and communicating with Him through intercession.

We must also know the scripture. As I have taught young men and women over the years, I have asked them to picture the tragedy of coming to the end of this age and having all kinds of gifts of the Holy Spirit but little knowledge of the bible. What if they knew how to encounter God but didn't know how to interpret God's activity and anchor it in God's Word? There is no shortcut to serious study of the Bible.

3). What is our Means?

Ten of the most important words in the Bible are found in John 20:21: *"As the Father has sent me, I am sending you."*

According to Philippians 2, Jesus emptied Himself when He came to earth as a man. He didn't hold on to what was rightfully His. He ministered with signs and wonders, but the means of His power was the Holy Spirit. It is the same for us. We have access to the same means of ministry that He had. That is why He could promise us that we would do greater works!

Know the message, embrace the mission, surrender to the means of the Holy Spirit. This is how you can be locked and loaded in this commission.

Bible Study

You must really be getting the hang of this SMART Bible study. Isn't the Word of God amazing?

Psalm 2
Matthew 28
John 1
Philippians 2

Vintage Poetry – "Take My Life"

Take my life and let it be
Consecrated, Lord, to Thee.
Take my moments and my days,
Let them flow in endless praise.

Take my hands and let them move
At the impulse of Thy love.
Take my feet and let them be
Swift and beautiful for Thee.

Take my voice and let me sing,
Always, only for my King.
Take my lips and let them be
Filled with messages from Thee.

Take my silver and my gold,
Not a mite would I withhold.
Take my intellect and use
Every pow'r as Thou shalt choose.

Take my will and make it Thine,
It shall be no longer mine.
Take my heart, it is Thine own,
It shall be Thy royal throne.

Take my love, my Lord, I pour
At Thy feet its treasure store.
Take myself and I will be
Ever, only, all for Thee.

Frances R. Havergal – 1874

Creative Space

Chapter Eight: Ascension and Anticipation

This is our last week to study The 40 Days of Easter. We've looked at the following themes:

Reality of Resurrection

Heart for the Hopeless

Searching the Scripture

Dispelling the Doubt

Peace through Proof

Road to Restoration

Command and Commission

We've seen the things that were on Christ's heart prior to Him physically leaving the planet. And through the witness of the Holy Spirit, we have experienced that they are still on His heart today. He is moving among us and still focusing on these themes.

As we close this study, we are going to look at both the ascension of Jesus and some promises that were made just before His body lifted up into the clouds. I hope that we catch the same level of anticipation that must have filled the hearts of Christ's followers. And here's the biggest goal of this study…

I hope that you receive the same power that came from heaven. I hope that you have Pentecost.

Before we look at three facts about Christ's ascension and three events for anticipation, take a look at these three passages of scripture: Mark 16:19,20; Luke 24:50-52; and Acts 1:1-11.

Three Facts of Christ's Ascension

#1 – Jesus ascended to the Father

I love to picture the ascension. Those that followed Jesus saw some amazing things: the blind saw, the lame walked, the storm calmed, etc. But certainly one of the most amazing was the day that Jesus' feet left the ground.

It was forty days after the resurrection. After some crucial dialogue we will look at later in this study, it happened. One moment, the disciples were looking at Christ eye to eye. . .

The next moment, they were having to raise their heads upward. His feet were not touching the ground! His body was lifting off! I wonder if Peter tried to grab His leg like you might reach out for the string of a balloon that has gotten away?

He ascended into the sky until a cloud hid Him from their sight. Amazing.

I wonder what the next scene was like for Jesus? You've probably seen some great reunions. I just witnessed one at the airport yesterday. You can picture it:

There's a weary traveler coming home and an anxious family at the airport gate. Sometimes there are gifts and banners welcoming the sojourner. The crowd waits and watches for the one that they love. When the traveler's face appears, there are yelps of delight, tears and embraces. The loved one is home.

What was this heavenly reunion like? When Jesus arrived, did an angelic conductor strike up the heavenly band? Was there a welcome banner inscribed by the very finger of God? Thirty three years before, Jesus left the splendor of heaven. He emptied Himself of what was rightfully His to come to a stable, sawdust, sleeplessness and sacrifice. But now, He returned home. He returned to His Father. The plan of redemption and reconciliation set in place before the foundation of the earth was finished. The Lamb returned victorious.

This reunion with the Father happened in a throne room. The scripture is clear, Jesus ascended to a place at the right hand of the Father. The imagery certainly denotes authority, kingly power, divinity.

Christ's incarnation (taking on the flesh of humanity) culminated on a cross. Jesus became the perfect human sacrifice for the sin of the world. Christ's resurrection culminated on a throne. From a position of power at the right hand of the Father, Jesus rules over the earth far above every evil power.

#2 – Jesus ascended with flesh

This may not seem like a big deal, but it is. When Jesus took on flesh and entered into the womb of Mary, He took on flesh forever. When He ascended into heaven,

He did not return just like He was before. He didn't go back to being God again after a short stint of being man. He went back to the Father fully God and now fully man.

Look at this beautiful quote from John Wesley:

"Jesus is still wearing those tokens of His passion on His dazzling body."

Christ's commitment to fully identify with humankind is not only full, it is forever. Right now, there is a nail-scarred human being sitting on a throne ruling over the earth and interceding for us.

If we don't embrace the truth of the ascension, we can place too much emphasis on the Church and move into a puffed up triumphalism.

Jesus didn't leave with His fingers crossed hoping that the Church will succeed. He's not standing back stage waiting to return to clean up any mess that we might make while He was gone. Right now, Jesus is center stage, He's at the helm. His is fully in charge and fully engaged. He has a plan and a purpose and He has not missed a beat.

Every time He lifts His human hand, all of heaven can see from the scar how deeply He cares for this world. That hand is the hand of God. That hand shows that God is for us. That hand will have skin on it forever.

#3 – Jesus ascends as a forerunner

Every step you take with Jesus is fueled by grace. Before you knew Christ as your Savior, you were drawn to Him by *prevenient* grace; grace that goes before. God is always the initiator. We love Him because He first loved us.

At the moment of your salvation, you experienced *justifying* grace. By God's grace you were cleansed of all sin and made righteous before God.

From that moment, you began receiving *sanctifying* grace. God did not just want you released from the penalty of your sin, He wants you released from the power of sin. Through His grace you can live holy.

There is coming a day when each of us who love Jesus will encounter *glorifying* grace. We will be transformed and we will receive a resurrected body. In Philippians 3, we are given the promise that *when He appears, we will be like Him!"*

Jesus has gone ahead of us. He has prepared the way. He is functioning in a glorified body just like one He will give to each of us one day. He is, again, the great pioneer of our faith. He is our forerunner.

Three Events for Anticipation

#1 – The Restoration of Israel – Acts 1:6

Just before Jesus ascended into heaven, the disciples asked an important question: *"Lord, are you at this time going to restore the kingdom to Israel?"*

God's plan and purpose for Israel is as relevant today as it was over 2,000 years ago. Unfortunately, much of the Church has lost touch with core biblical truth regarding God's promise to the Jewish people. Many in the Church have embraced what is called "replacement theology." This is the idea that the Church has replaced Israel. In other words, all of the promises made to Israel are now realized by those who are Christian. We have become a "spiritual Israel."

Here is a good way to look at the Bible: It means what it says and it says what it means.

Israel is a nation set apart by God to be a witness to the world of God's activity on the earth. She is the recipient of eternal covenants with God. Look at the words of Paul in Romans 9: *"Theirs (Israel) is the adoption as sons; theirs the divine glory, the covenants, the receiving of the law, temple worship and the promises. Theirs are the patriarchs, and from them is traced the human ancestry of Christ, who is God over all, forever praised! Amen."*

God is a keeper of promises. Israel is the main branch in God's world-wide vineyard. Those of us who are Gentile believers have the privilege of being grafted in. (Romans 10:17) And we have a job to do. The Bible says that one of the reasons that salvation has come to Gentiles is to make Israel envious. (Romans 11:11) The Bible also promises that there is a great move of God coming for Israel. In Romans chapter 11, God describes the number of Gentile believers reaching a full number on the earth and then He will come to Israel: *"The deliverer will come from Zion; he will turn godlessness away from Jacob. And this is my covenant with them when I take away their sins."*

In 1948, one of the great miracles of God took place. Israel was restored as a nation on the very land that God promised to them centuries before. Do you realize how amazing this is? Think about it. Israel, like many other people groups in the Bible, was defeated and scattered from their homeland across the earth. But for 2,000 years, they kept their traditions, their language, and their culture. And they held on to their promises from God.

In God's time, they came from the four corners of the earth and repopulated the promised land. Astounding. Can you imagine the Hittites doing this?

The world is primed. The Bible says what it means and means what it says. Israel is back on their promised land. There is a day coming when Jesus Himself will restore God's Kingdom to Israel.

#2 – The Coming of the Holy Spirit with Power – Acts 1:8

The last words of Jesus before He went up, up and away were: *"You will receive power when the Holy Spirit comes on you; and you will be my witnesses in Jerusalem, and in all Judea and Samaria, and to the ends of the earth."*

What highly charged words. Literally. The Greek word that is translated "power" is *dunamis*. That's the root from which we get the word dynamite! Jesus is promising an explosion of power. And the disciples are told to wait for it. They waited for 10 days. Can you imagine the building anticipation?

For 40 days, Jesus gave His followers many convincing proofs that He was alive. (Acts 1:3) Before He ascended, He convinced them to wait in Jerusalem for an outpouring of power through the Holy Spirit. And they believed.

While together in an upstairs room, the promise was fulfilled. It started with an out of this world sound, like the rushing wind. Then fire appeared over each of their heads. Soon what was external became internal; they were filled with the Holy Spirit. And finally, they began to speak in a language previously unknown to them.

The Holy Spirit was now inside of them. The same source that fueled the ministry of Jesus was accessible to each of them. That is why Jesus could promise them that they would do greater things. And the first fruit of this new way of living was 3,000 new believers in Jesus Christ in just one day!

It gets even better. The Holy Spirit was poured out again in Acts 4. And again in Acts 10. It wasn't just a onetime thing. In fact, Acts 28 ends abruptly. There is no resolution. . .

Because the story of a Holy Spirit empowered Church hasn't ended.

There may be a chapter to be written as you gather with friends for this week's study!

#3 – The return of Christ the King – Acts 1:11

Jesus ascended and the disciples were obviously gawking. Like a crowd watching the space shuttle, they were locked in on Jesus as He disappeared into the clouds. Two angels appeared to them with a challenging word: *Get your head out of the clouds! This man who you saw go up today will come back down in the same way!*

That word became one of the most often repeated themes in the New Testament. At the end of his life, Peter wrote: *"But do not forget this one thing, dear friends. . .the Day of the Lord will come. . . "* (2 Peter 3:8,10)

John wrote to his children in the faith: *"Continue in him so that when he appears we may be confident and unashamed before him at his coming."* I John 2:28

And Paul exhorted: *"For the Lord himself will come down from heaven, with a loud command, with the voice of the archangel and with the trumpet call of God. . ."* I Thessalonians 4:15

Before Jesus ascended into heaven, He gave us three things to anticipate: The restoration of Israel, the coming of the Holy Spirit with power and His triumphant return.

How are these realities impacting your life today?

Bible Study

Let the wild, creative Holy Spirit move in your mind as you study and write things down to share with your friends.

Acts 1,2
Philippians 3
Romans 10,11
I Thessalonians 4

Vintage Poetry – "Come Thou Long Expected Jesus"

Come, Thou long expected Jesus
Born to set Thy people free;
From our fears and sins release us,
Let us find our rest in Thee.

Israel's Strength and Consolation,
Hope of all the earth Thou art;
Dear Desire of every nation,
Joy of every longing heart.

Born Thy people to deliver,
Born a child and yet a King,
Born to reign in us forever,
Now Thy gracious kingdom bring.

By Thine own eternal Spirit
Rule in all our hearts alone;
By Thine all sufficient merit,
Raise us to Thy glorious throne.

Charles Wesley -- 1745

Creative Space

_____

_____

_____

_____

_____

_____

_____

_____

_____

_____

_____

_____

SMART Bible Reading

There are few things more important in the Christian life than reading the Bible. It is God's primary way of speaking to us. The Bible is one of a kind. It has authority, it is inspired, it is alive with the very breath of God. And it is crucial that we know it so that we can be effective witnesses of God's activity on the earth. The stakes are very high as we get closer to the end of this age. Imagine the tragedy of being saved, even filled with the Holy Spirit with gifts and graces, but you cannot walk people through the truth of God's plan and purpose because you have not studied God's Word.

There are no short cuts. It takes time and commitment. I believe God wants us to wrestle with His truth. It's good to listen to others talk about the Bible. It's important to read how others interpret the Bible. But do not be satisfied with pre-digested food. Open your Bible daily, it is a banquet set for you and the special guest at your table will be the Holy Spirit.

Below is a simple plan for your Bible reading. Would you spend this next year asking the Lord to help you engage the Bible in each of these five ways? It's a SMART thing to do.

S – Study

Read the Bible systematically. Go online and find one of the plans to read the Bible through in a year. (The website for Discipleship Journal has my favorite. I used it for 10 straight years and the Lord blessed my study.) It's really good to use some great study tools like commentaries, but spend most of your time in the Bible. Don't focus too much on pre-digested spiritual food!

M – Meditate

Read the Bible prayerfully. Realize that you are not alone. The same Spirit that inspired the words is with you. Talk to Him about what you read.

A – Apply

Read the Bible expectantly. It really is your source for faith (what you believe) and practice (how you should live).

R – Respond

Read the Bible actively. Before you close the cover, ask Jesus to give you a heads up regarding how you could walk it out that very day.

T – Teach

Read the Bible generously. Believe as you read that the Lord will reveal truth that is meant to be shared. Everyone of us should be looking for ways to invest what God gives us in the lives of others. Your kitchen table could become an altar where the presence of Jesus comes for a friend as you open the Word of Life.

About the Author

Rich is the Director of The Malachi Network
(www.malachinetwork.org), a ministry focused on making
the name of the LORD great among the nations. This
network serves 50+ young leaders in missions and church
planting around the globe.

Prior to his present ministry, Rich has pastored and
planted churches in NJ, KY and MO, established a global
network of churches, taught at Asbury University,
International House of Prayer University and Bethany
College of Mission, and served as a Missionary.

Rich is the author of three books:
**Secrets of the Spiritual Life—10 Lessons from the One
Thing Passages** (Baker Books, 2003)
**A Voice from Home—The Words You Long to Hear
from Your Father** (WaterBrook Press, 2005)
Let's Dance – A New Way of Relating to Jesus
(1elevenmedia, 2017)

He graduated from Asbury University in 1984 with a BA
degree in Philosophy of Religion and Asbury Theological
Seminary in 1987 with a Master of Divinity degree. In
2010, Rich received an honorary Doctor of Divinity degree
from Union Biblical Seminary in Yangon, Myanmar.

Rich has been married to Tania since 1982 and they have
been blessed by amazing children and grandchildren:
Zachary, his wife Meghan and daughter, Naima, Jacob, his
wife Lena and sons, Grey and Levi, Jessica and Corrie
Emma.

If you are interested in having Rich speak at your event,
contact him at: richstevenson63@gmail.com.

Made in the USA
Coppell, TX
23 March 2024

30444459R00059